10/98

24 26

The
MEDITERRANEAN SEA

David Lambert

RSVP
RAINTREE
STECK-VAUGHN
P U B L I S H E R S
The Steck-Vaughn Company

Austin, Texas

Seas and Oceans series

The Atlantic Ocean
The Caribbean and the Gulf of Mexico
The Indian Ocean
The Mediterranean Sea
The North Sea and the Baltic Sea
The Pacific Ocean
The Polar Seas
The Red Sea and the Arabian Gulf

Cover: A view of the Dalmatian coast, Dubrovnik, Herzegovina

Published by Raintree Steck-Vaughn Publishers,
an imprint of Steck-Vaughn Company

Library of Congress Cataloging-in-Publication Data
Lambert, David.
The mediterranean sea / David Lambert.
 p. cm.—(Seas and oceans)
Includes bibliographical references and index.
Summary: Examines the geography, plants, animals, trade, and resources of the Mediterranean Sea
ISBN 0-8172-4512-X
1. Mediterranean sea—Juvenile literature.
[1. Mediterranean sea.]
I. Title. II. Series: Seas and oceans (Austin, Tex.)
GC651.L36 1997
551.46'2—dc20   96-31163

Printed in Italy. Bound in the United States.
1 2 3 4 5 6 7 8 9 0 01 00 99 98 97

Picture acknowledgments:
Dieter Betz 40; Bridgeman Art Library 18, 26 (British Library); Britstock IFA *cover* (C. L. Schmitt); CEPHAS 44 (Mick Rock); Bruce Coleman 17 (Hans Reinhard), 32 Atlantide SDF); James Davis Travel Photography 22, 25, 28; Ecoscene 7, 30 (Andrew Brown), 39 (Wilkinson), 45 (Mark Laney); Eye Ubiquitous 11 (TRIP), 37 (BB Pictures), 42 (Selby); Ole Steen Hansen 33; Frank Lane Picture Agencey 12 (D. P. Wilson), 14 (James D. Watt/Earthviews), 16 (Roger Tidman), 20–21 (bottom/John Hawkins), 38 (Silvestris), 43 (E. & D. Hosking); Life File 21 (top/Sue Davies), 23 (inset/Graham Buchan), 34 (Guy Usher), 35 (Juliet Highet); Medimage 5, 23 (left), 27; Oxford Scientific Films 13 (Paul Kay), 15 (R. L. Manuel); Panos Pictures 24 (J. C. Tordai); Science Photo Library 31 (Occidental Consortium); Tony Stone Worldwide 36 (Hugh Sitton), 41 (Simeone Huber); Julia Waterlow 8, 9; Zefa 29 (Mueller).
All artwork is supplied by Hardlines.

Contents

Words that appear in **bold** in the text can be found in
the glossary on page 46.

INTRODUCTION
"In the Middle of the Land"

The Mediterranean Sea is one of the world's largest seas. It is famous for clear blue water, almost no tides, and the ancient civilizations that stood on its shores. Once, it was much bigger than it is now and wide open, to the north and south. Today, it is almost completely surrounded by land. In fact, the name *Mediterranean* comes from the Latin word meaning "in the middle of the land."

Most of the Mediterranean lies between Europe to the north, Africa to the south, and Asia to the east. Only narrow passages connect it to other great masses of water. In the west, the **Strait** of Gibraltar joins the Mediterranean to the Atlantic Ocean. Another strait, the Dardanelles, links the Mediterranean to the Black Sea in the northeast. In the southeast, the Suez Canal connects it with the Red Sea.

The Mediterranean is five times longer than its average width. It measures about 2,200 miles from Spain in the west to Syria in the east. At its broadest, it measures only about

Below: The Mediterranean Sea is almost completely enclosed by land. This map shows some of the islands and bordering nations of the Mediterranean.

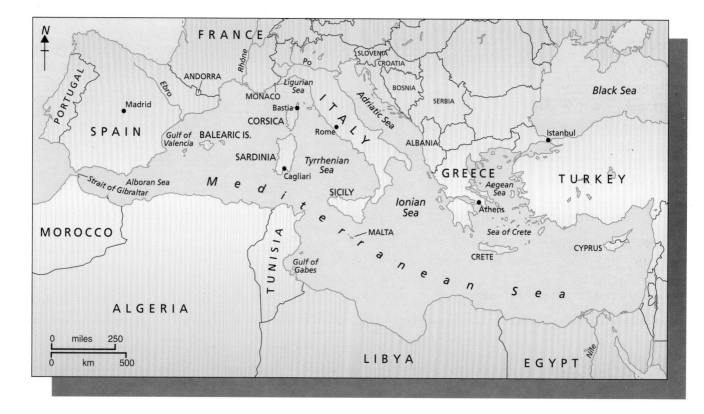

4

800 miles from Libya in the south to Montenegro in the north. From west to east, large islands stand spaced out rather like stepping-stones. These islands and peninsulas jutting down from the north help divide much of the northern Mediterranean into five smaller seas. From west to east, these are the Ligurian Sea, Tyrrhenian Sea, Adriatic Sea, Ionian Sea, and the Aegean Sea. Some people also think of the Sea of Marmara and the Black Sea beyond it as part of the Mediterranean.

Long ago, civilizations sprang up on Mediterranean coasts. It became one of the ancient world's great water highways for trade and migration. Today, cargo ships use the sea as a shortcut between Asia and Europe. Its fish and shellfish help feed the area's peoples, and warmth-loving food crops grow near its coasts. Each summer, millions of vacationers visit its hot, sunny shores. But the Mediterranean suffers more heavily from **pollution** than most other seas. Cleaning it up is a big problem for the surrounding countries.

Above: You can easily see across the Strait of Gibraltar from Spain to Morocco. Only 10 miles of water separates Europe from Africa, at the western end of the Mediterranean.

PHYSICAL GEOGRAPHY
Sea Floor and Coasts

Off most Mediterranean coasts lies a shallow **continental shelf** far narrower than the continental shelf around most oceans. Beyond this, the seabed slopes down to a complicated jumble of basins, deep troughs, and underwater ridges. The biggest, highest ridge runs from Tunisia to Sicily. This ridge almost cuts the sea in half and divides the sea floor into two main basins.

The western basin is largely made of abyssal (deepsea) plains, though some have smoother floors than others. The western basin's lowest point, in the Tyrrhenian Sea, is 12,000 feet deep. The eastern basin is bigger and more rugged than the western basin and reaches even greater depths. Its floor is largely made of underwater ridges and trenches. Off southwest Greece lies water more than 16,400 feet deep—deeper than anywhere else in the Mediterranean.

There are thousands of Mediterranean islands, although most of them are tiny. The largest island, Sicily, rises from

Below: The floor of the Mediterranean Sea is a rugged landscape of mountains and trenches.

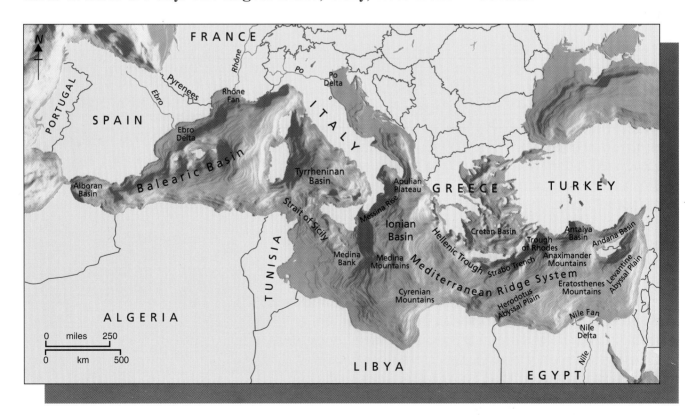

the ridge between the sea's western and eastern basins. The western basin's largest islands are Sardinia, Corsica, and the Balearic Islands. The largest islands of the eastern basin are Cyprus, Crete, and Euboea. The eastern basin is where most small islands stand. Many make up rows or clusters. These include the Ionian Islands in the Ionian Sea and the Cyclades, Sporades, and Dodecanese in the Aegean Sea. In the southern Aegean and off southwest Italy some islands are volcanic. Indeed, Mount Etna on Sicily is Europe's tallest active volcano.

Along much of the Mediterranean, rugged hills or mountains rise sharply from the sea or from a narrow coastal plain. Where mountains rise abruptly from the water, rocky peninsulas, bays, and inlets make the coastline zigzag in and out sharply. This happens where the Pyrenees, Alps, and other mountain ranges come right down to the sea. But broad plains reach the sea in Libya and Egypt. Also, the big rivers—Ebro in Spain, Rhône in France, Po in Italy, and Nile in Egypt—have built fan-shaped aprons of low muddy land, called deltas, out into the sea.

Above: Snow-capped Mount Etna looms beyond the buildings of Taormina in Sicily. Rising 11,122 ft. above sea level, Europe's tallest active volcano dominates the Mediterranean's largest island.

How big and how deep?	
Area	1,144,876 sq. mi.
Average water depth	4,921 ft.
Maximum water depth	16,706 ft. (Hellenic Trough)

How the Sea Took Shape

Slow shifting by giant slabs of the earth's **crust** formed the Mediterranean's crumpled floor, its islands, and the mountains around its rim.

Two main **tectonic plates**, or slabs of crust, have been involved. One includes Africa and part of the Mediterranean sea floor. The other plate contains Europe and much of Asia. The African plate is drifting north toward the Eurasian plate. Over millions of years, this movement has squeezed great areas of rock. They crumpled to build the mountain ranges of northwest Africa and southern Europe. Meanwhile, slabs of crust broke off from the two main plates and jostled around. Parts of Spain and Africa moved east and came together, forming Italy and Sicily. More pieces trailed behind as the islands of Sardinia and Corsica.

Farther east, the seabed has been squashed where the Ionian, Aegean, and Turkish plates were squeezed between the Eurasian plate to the north and the African and Arabian plates to the south. Deep, seabed trenches show where the Ionian plate dives under the Aegean plate. Some of this rock lost inside the earth melted and bobbed up through the Aegean plate to build the south Aegean's curved row of

Below: Cliffs rim a vast crater that formed and filled with sea when a big volcanic island blew off its top. Thera is a Greek volcanic island in the Aegean Sea.

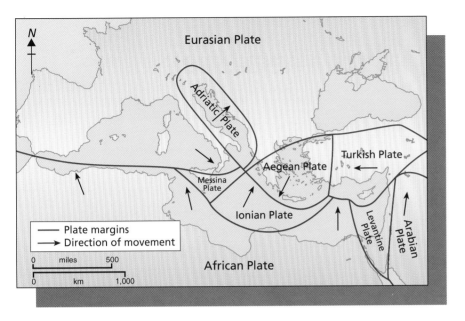

Left: This map shows the movement of the main tectonic plates. They have pushed together to form the islands, mountains, and trenches of the region.

volcanic islands. To their north, plate movements have created other islands.

These changes caused shores to rise and fall around the Mediterranean. In the last 2,000 years, hundreds of seaside towns have drowned. Yet eastern Italy and western Crete have risen.

Far greater sea level changes happened 6 million years ago when Africa touched Spain and shut out the Atlantic Ocean. The Mediterranean almost dried up. Only its deepest hollows still held pools of water, and the Nile and Rhône rivers cut **canyons** far down to reach the new, low sea level. There was more salt than the sea could hold, so salt layers up to 1 mile thick piled up on the seabed. When the Atlantic Ocean burst in again, the Mediterranean refilled. But thick salt layers still lie on its floor.

Earthquakes and erupting volcanoes suggest that plate movements are still going on. One day, these plate movements may squeeze the Mediterranean shut for good.

A giant explosion

In 1628 B.C., the volcanic island of Thera, or Santorini, north of Crete blew up. It was as though lots of hydrogen bombs had been set off at once. Scientists think this was the biggest bang since civilization began. People living all around the Mediterranean probably heard it. The explosion happened because gases slowly collected in a chamber under the volcano. Their pressure increased until it blew off Thera's top. All that now remains of the big island is a ring of small ones surrounding a great cavity full of seawater. In the middle, new volcanoes have begun to rise.

PHYSICAL GEOGRAPHY
Water, Winds, and Weather

The Mediterranean Sea is like a bath being emptied as fast as it fills. Most of the water that flows in comes from the Atlantic Ocean and the Black Sea. Rivers also pour water into the Mediterranean. The biggest of them are the Ebro, the Rhône, the Po, and the Nile.

Meanwhile, the Mediterranean is emptying. Huge amounts of water evaporate into the air as water vapor, especially in summer. Each year, enough water to form a layer 5 feet deep evaporates from the sea's hot eastern end. In addition, cold, heavy water escapes into the Atlantic Ocean. This water flows out through the Strait of Gibraltar below the warmer, less salty, lighter water flowing in.

Surface water temperatures and salinity	
Surface temperatures	53–68°F (western basin) 55–80°F (eastern basin)
Bottom temperatures	55.6°F (western basin) 56.5°F (eastern basin)
Salinity (parts per thousand)	36.3 (western surface) 39.0 (eastern surface)

Water entering and leaving the Mediterranean helps keep **currents** moving through its surface. These flow counterclockwise around the sea. Most currents, however, are weak. In summer, warm, light surface water does not mix with the colder, heavier water below. In winter, though, both layers mingle where winds stir up the surface. Unlike other oceans, this almost shut-off sea has no noticeable tides. On most shores the sea level rises and falls less than 3 feet every day.

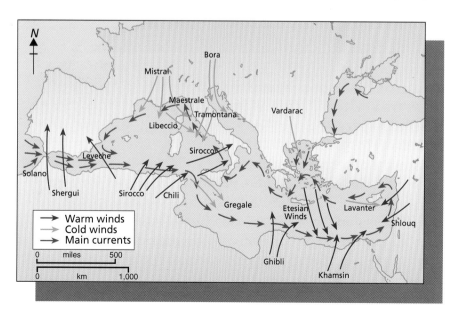

Left: The Mediterranean Sea has a complex circulation pattern of currents and warm and cold winds.

Sometimes, though, winds send storm waves breaking high on the shore. In various parts of the sea, strong winds blow from special directions at certain times of year. The wildest time is winter, when unsettled weather arrives from the Atlantic. Then **depressions** track east, bringing dull, rainy, windy conditions. The fierce, cold **mistral** wind may blow down the Rhône valley. But mountains, including the Alps, shield the northern Mediterranean from most cold winds, and summer warmth stored in its water helps keep coasts too mild for frost to form. In summer, depressions give way to **anticyclones**. These high-pressure air masses bring settled weather that is hot, dry, and sunny. Wherever it occurs in the world, this pattern of mild, wet winters and hot, dry summers is known as a "Mediterranean climate."

Above: North Africa's hot, dry sirocco wind blows the tops off these waves. The sirocco can scorch grape vines and dump the Sahara's dust as far away as southern Europe.

Food Chains and Marine Plants

Mediterranean plants and animals have Atlantic Ocean ancestors. These came in when the Atlantic refilled the almost empty Mediterranean millions of years ago.

Tiny organisms arrive all the time, with the current flowing past Gibraltar. Most are one-celled **algae** living in the sunlit surface waters. These form the plant **plankton**. Among them live tiny one-celled animals, called protozoans, and lots of shrimplike creatures, together with the young stages of many bigger animals, such as crabs, sea urchins, and fish. All these little creatures make up the animal plankton.

Each kind of alga forms the start of a food chain. An alga might be eaten by a protozoan. The protozoan could be gobbled up by a tiny shrimp and the shrimp swallowed by a young fish. The young fish might become food for a sardine. The sardine could be snapped up by a mackerel. The mackerel might end up inside a swordfish. The swordfish could be caught by fishermen and served on people's plates. Similar food chains occur throughout the world's oceans. Each kind of creature in a food chain might eat and be eaten by several other kinds. In this way, separate food chains link up to form a more complicated **food web**.

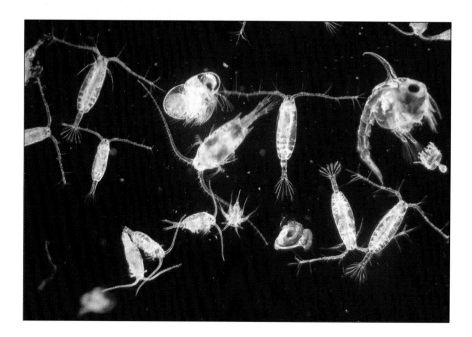

Left: In this magnified picture of animal plankton the "knight's helmet" is a baby crab, and the creatures with two long antennae are copepods. A copepod is almost too small to be seen, yet in one day it might eat 120,000 even smaller organisms called diatoms.

Besides tiny floating algae in the open sea, the Mediterranean also has large algae, called seaweeds, with rootlike holdfasts that grip the rocky floors of shallow inshore waters. The Mediterranean is warmer than waters farther north, so warmth-loving red seaweeds are more plentiful than the brown seaweeds you find mainly in cooler waters.

Even flowering plants thrive in the Mediterranean. Sea grasses grow in shallow and muddy areas. In some places, the narrow, strap-shaped leaves of *Posidonia* form underwater meadows. *Posidonia* produces tiny flowers. Their pollen drifts about in shallow water, fertilizing the seeds. Sea grasses flourish off Mediterranean shores because the tide does not go out far enough to let their fragile leaves dry out and die. But storm waves can snap them off. Then dead, brown leaves wash up on the shore to build thick heaps that look like giant mattresses.

Above: This underwater sea grass meadow grows off Gozo, a small island belonging to Malta. Pipefishes hide among the leaves, and sea turtles eat them.

Invertebrates and Fish

As in all seas and oceans, in the Mediterranean different creatures live at various depths. Fewer kinds of deepsea creatures live here than in the Atlantic, though. This is because some never managed to cross its shallow threshold.

Many Mediterranean seabed animals feed on dead and dying organisms that drift down from above. Bottom-dwelling **invertebrates** include plantlike sponges and soft corals. There are also sea worms, and **mollusks**, from octopuses that hide in rock crannies, to a remarkable sea snail. People once prized this snail because it yielded a purple dye used for coloring emperors' robes. Among the Mediterranean **crustaceans** are various crabs, shrimps, and lobsters. One small kind of lobster is eaten as scampi. Parts of the seabed

Below: A swordfish is a large, streamlined hunter. Its sword is not much shorter than its body, which often grows 6.5 feet long.

An octopus creeps from a sea-bed cranny to hunt. Eight tentacles armed with suckers seize fish and bring them to its beak-shaped mouth.

teem with echinoderms (invertebrates with spiny skins), especially sea cucumbers and a kind of black sea urchin that bristles with long, sharp spines.

Bottom-living algae or invertebrates provide food for various Mediterranean seabed fish. Plaice, skates, and rays are flatfish that lie and feed on a soft, sandy floor. Thick-lipped gray mullets strain food from the muddy bottoms of harbors and estuaries. Long, thin pipefish hide among sea grasses. Red mullets, wrasses, and scorpion fish swim and lurk among rocks.

The gloomy middle depths of the open sea are home to squid and blue sharks. Nearly 200 glowing light organs make one kind of Mediterranean squid show up in the dark.

The sea creatures that people most often see are those that live near the surface. Here, the best-known invertebrates are jellyfish, such as the Mediterranean sea wasp, so-called because of its poisonous stings. Sardines, anchovies, mackerel, and flying fish form schools of fish millions strong. To escape enemies, the little flying fish burst from the sea and skim the waves, gliding on long, wing-shaped side fins. Packs of large, fast tunas hunt the smaller fish. So do swordfish, slashing at nimble shoals with the long sword on their snout. Swordfish and tunas are great travelers. They come and go between the Mediterranean and the Atlantic.

Reptiles, Birds, and Mammals

Besides invertebrates and fish, the Mediterranean has swimming or diving reptiles, birds, and mammals.

Loggerhead turtles spend almost all their lives at sea, using their sharp, beak-like mouths to bite jellyfish, crabs, and underwater plants. Each year the females crawl ashore to lay their eggs on sandy beaches, especially in Libya, Greece, and Turkey. Sometimes, leatherback turtles swim in from the Atlantic, hunting jellyfish. At up to 6.5 ft. long and weighing 1,100 lbs., these are the world's largest turtles.

The Mediterranean lacks the huge seabird colonies found along northern oceans. This is because the sea holds fewer fish for birds to eat. But the Mediterranean has its share of gulls, terns, and shearwaters. Cory's shearwater breeds only in the Mediterranean, and Audouin's gull lives nowhere else.

Winged wayfarers

More birds fly over the Mediterranean than live on its water or shores. Most of these travelers are land birds. Each spring they migrate north to Europe and Asia to breed. Each autumn they come back with their young to spend winter in warm parts of Africa. At night, small songbirds fly across the sea on a broad front. Storks and eagles cross only by day. These broad-winged birds soar on rising air that has been warmed by the sun, then glide across narrow sea gaps where Europe almost touches Africa and Asia. Up to 5 billion birds pass over the Mediterranean each year.

Left: White storks migrate in large flocks over the Mediterranean.

Small wading birds run along the sandy beaches, and thousands of visiting waders spend winter here to escape cold, northern weather. Behind low shores, flocks of long-legged flamingos feed in shallow salty lakes, especially in part of southern France called the Camargue.

Rocky Greek and Turkish coasts are breeding grounds for Europe's rarest mammal: the Mediterranean monk seal. Monk seals are the only seals found in seas as warm as this. They usually appear in ones or twos, not in herds like other seals.

The sea's largest mammals are certain great whales. Fin whales and minke whales sometimes swim in from the Atlantic. These baleen whales trap plankton on fringed "combs" hanging from the roofs of their vast open mouths. Among toothed whales, the largest are the sperm whales, up to 60 ft. long. Their huge heads make these easy to identify. Sperm whales dive deeply after squid and octopus. Pilot whales and killer whales only reach the western Mediterranean. Its most plentiful and widespread whales are the small kinds called bottlenosed and common dolphins. Hundreds, even thousands, swim together, chasing schools of little fish and leaping from the sea.

Above: Mediterranean monk seals breed in quiet coves in the eastern Mediterranean. Only a few hundred of these mammals survive, and they are becoming more scarce.

MEDITERRANEAN PEOPLES
Early Inhabitants

People have lived by the Mediterranean for hundreds of thousands of years. Its eastern end was where Western civilization began.

The earliest inhabitants were **Stone Age** hunters of wild beasts, and gatherers of wild plants. *Homo erectus* probably arrived first. This type of human reached the east Mediterranean area from Africa more than 1.5 million years ago. By 100,000 years ago, strong, stocky **Neanderthal** people and humans like us both lived in what is now Israel. Later, the modern humans learned to make fine stone and bone weapons and tools. They also drew lifelike animal pictures on cave walls in France and Spain. Neanderthals lived there too, but died out by 30,000 years ago. By then, humans like us flourished right around the Mediterranean region.

By 9,000 years ago, Stone Age people near the eastern end of the Mediterranean became among the world's first to raise sheep, goats, and cattle as living larders. Others had already become some of the earliest farmers, growing wheat in fertile river valleys. Guaranteed food supplies allowed farmers to settle down and to live in one place. At places such as Çatal

Left: An artist painted wild cattle on a Spanish cave wall about 13,500 years ago. Spears and arrows helped Stone Age hunters kill such big animals for food.

Above: Ancient Egyptians built this pyramid as a tomb for King Khafre (Cheops). About 2500 B.C., tens of thousands of workers cut and raised its blocks of stone.

Hüyük in Turkey and Jericho in Jordan, their mud houses grew into some of the world's first villages and towns.

By 5,000 years ago, many towns grew into cities where river valleys produced harvests large enough to feed many thousands of people. In cities such as Memphis in Egypt, craftsmen made bronze tools and architects designed splendid tombs, temples, and palaces. The largest **Bronze Age** buildings were Egypt's pyramids. In Malta and Italy, however, Stone Age peoples had built great stone tombs and temples even earlier. Powerful Bronze Age rulers controlled the cities and the farms that fed them. Egypt's kings, called pharaohs, also led powerful armies. War helped Egypt win one of the world's first empires.

By 3,500 years ago, other Bronze Age powers also flourished at the eastern end of the Mediterranean: Mycenaeans in Greece, Minoans in Crete, Hittites in Turkey, and **Phoenician** cities on coasts now in Syria, Lebanon, and Israel.

Iron Age Colonies and Empires

About 3,500 years ago, the Hittites in Turkey learned to make iron tools and weapons. Iron was more plentiful than the copper and tin used in bronze, so it was cheaper. Almost anyone could afford iron tools or weapons. The Mediterranean now entered an **Iron Age,** when its peoples formed colonies and empires, and Western civilization truly began.

Greek farmers using iron tools produced extra food that nourished a growing population. At last, though, there were more Greeks than the land could feed. Thousands found new

Right: The Parthenon at Athens is the best-known Greek temple. Copying Greek designs, the Romans later built fine stone temples right around the Mediterranean.

Below: A Roman road winds through Spain's Gredos Mountains. On low ground it would have run quite straight. Firm roads carried goods and troops all over the Roman Empire.

homes abroad. Greek **colonists** set up towns and cities around the Black Sea and on Mediterranean coasts as far west as Italy and France. Phoenician traders had already sailed west from what are now Syria, Lebanon, and Israel. The Phoenicians founded their own Mediterranean settlements in North Africa, Sicily, Sardinia, and Spain.

Meanwhile, iron spears helped Asian armies win empires at the sea's eastern end. From what is now Iraq came the Assyrians, then the Babylonians. Later still, Persia (now called Iran) won an empire that stretched from India to Egypt and Greece.

A Greek army led by Alexander the Great conquered the Persian Empire by 331 B.C. The Greeks produced fine sculptures, buildings, paintings, plays, poetry, music, and new ideas about mathematics, medicine, astronomy, government, and philosophy. Alexander's Hellenistic Empire spread Greek civilization abroad.

But empires also appeared in the western Mediterranean. By 500 B.C. much of North Africa and Spain was controlled by Carthage, a North African city founded by the Phoenicians. The Carthaginians' main rivals were the Romans of Italy. In 202 B.C. the Romans defeated the Carthaginians. The Romans won the eastern Mediterranean too. For hundreds of years, the Roman Empire ruled the whole region. Rome became the world's first city with more than a million inhabitants, and Roman roads, canals, and public buildings sprang up the length of the Mediterranean.

Western civilization began in Greece, but the Romans spread it throughout the Mediterranean. At the sea's eastern end, the Roman province of Judaea was where Christianity began.

Peoples on the Move

The Roman empire broke up by A.D. 500. For the next 1,000 years the Mediterranean Sea and its shores were routes for armies, sea raiders, and migrants. Indeed, most Jews had emigrated even before A.D. 100, when the Romans punished a Jewish revolt by destroying the Jewish capital, Jerusalem.

By A.D. 500 northern European peoples had overrun the western half of the Roman Empire. Different groups of so-called **barbarians** seized or settled in almost every part of southern Europe. The group called Vandals even formed a kingdom in North Africa. In time, though, the various kingdoms shared one religion—Christianity.

From the east came armies of Muslims, believers in the faith called Islam. Soon after A.D. 700, Arab Muslims ruled most of the southern Mediterranean including Spain, North Africa, and Egypt. By the late 1400s, Turkish Muslims had seized Turkey and southeast Europe from the Byzantine Empire—the eastern remains of the old Roman Empire.

The Krak des Chevaliers (castle of knights) stands in Syria. A crusading army built its massive walls and towers more than 800 years ago.

Left: Spain's Muslim invaders designed the Alhambra at Granada as a palace fortress.

Above: Inside the Alhambra, fountains stand in courtyards with delicate columns and arches.

Europe's Christian rulers became the Muslims' enemies. Between A.D. 1096 and 1291, Christian expeditions called **crusades** attacked the Muslims occupying Palestine, the Christians' Holy Land. These crusades failed. Christian armies retook Spain by 1492, but Muslim pirates seized European ships and raided European ports.

Meanwhile, the Mediterranean region provided more than paths for armies. New food crops and ideas passed through from east to west. Muslim Arabs introduced Eastern food such as rice, sugarcane, oranges, and peaches as far west as Spain and Portugal. From Muslim scholars, Europeans learned forgotten knowledge of the ancient Greeks. The Chinese invention of gunpowder and Arabic numerals (the Indian way of writing numbers that we use today) reached Europe by way of the Mediterranean. And in Spain, Sicily, and Italy, artists and architects created palaces and churches beautifully decorated in the Arab style. Western civilization owes much to the ideas and inventions once kept alive in Mediterranean lands under Muslim Arab rule.

Mediterranean Peoples Today

People are spread unevenly around the Mediterranean. Much of Libya and Egypt is almost empty desert, with a few wandering herders and shepherds. Peasants tend small farms on the steep hillsides of Mediterranean Europe. Small fishing villages stand on rocky shores. But most people live on coastal plains and large river valleys, especially the valley of the Po in Italy and the Nile in Egypt. Many work in cities such as Barcelona in Spain, Marseilles in France, Milan and Naples in Italy, Athens in Greece, Istanbul in Turkey, Tel Aviv in Israel, Alexandria in Egypt, and Algiers in Algeria.

The Bosnian conflict

After World War I, small regions called Bosnia-Herzegovina, Croatia, Macedonia, Montenegro, Serbia, and Slovenia became one nation known as Yugoslavia. Various parts still had different religions and traditions, however. When Yugoslavia broke up in 1991, old differences and hatreds led to wars in certain areas, especially between the Christian Serbs and Muslim Bosnians who lived in Bosnia-Herzegovina. By the mid-1990s, United Nations troops had failed to prevent many thousands of villagers being driven from their homes and thousands of defenseless prisoners being massacred. This was the worst fighting seen in Europe since World War II.

Outside the cities, Mediterranean Europe's peasants earn less than the farmers of northern Europe. But the European Union provides money to help small farmers, especially in Spain, Italy, and Greece. This helps make them better off than the peasants of North Africa or Turkey. The average

Left: In this narrow Jerusalem street, women wear traditional clothes and shops display cheap goods in the open, as they have done for hundreds of years.

Left: People in fashionable clothes walk through a shopping arcade in the northern Italian city of Milan. The shops display expensive goods.

western European earns 75 percent more than most North Africans.

Mediterranean peoples are mainly descended from ancestors who settled there centuries ago. In southern Europe, Christianity is the chief religion, and Spaniards, French, and Italians speak languages that come from Latin, the language of the ancient Roman Empire. Most of North Africa's Arabs and Berbers are Muslims and speak Arabic. Elsewhere, Slavs, Greeks, Turks, and Jews have their own languages.

Old religious differences and others keep some groups at odds with one another. Between 1948 and 1967, the Jewish nation of Israel fought three wars with Arab neighbors. Since 1974, Cyprus has been divided between Greek and Turkish Cypriots. After Yugoslavia broke up in 1991, war broke out between its Croats, Serbs, and Muslims. In Algeria and Egypt, Muslims who want strict Islamic laws have killed Muslims who do not.

Since the early 1800s, war or poverty has driven millions of Mediterranean people to emigrate. Italians and Greeks often moved to North America or Australia. But Jews from all over the world moved to Israel after 1948, when that nation was created for them out of Palestine.

Ships and Shipping

Ships have sailed the Mediterranean for more than 4,000 years. Old paintings, models, and hundreds of sunken wrecks show how ships have changed through the ages.

The earliest seagoing ships appeared in the east. The Egyptians made boats from bundles of reeds. Phoenicians used wood. Both civilizations built ships that had masts with square sails and oars at the back for steering.

By 3,000 years ago, the Greeks had two main types of wooden crafts—warships and merchantmen. The warships were long, narrow vessels with sails and teams of oarsmen. These galleys had sharp prows for ramming enemy boats. Mediterranean sailors used oared warships similar to these until about four centuries ago.

Below: An old painting shows a Spanish galleon. A typical warship had a sharp prow, high forecastle, three or four masts with square and fore-and-aft sails, and guns along each side.

Early Mediterranean merchantmen were sailing ships with one square sail set crosswise and a broad, roomy hull for carrying cargo. Some Roman merchantmen weighed 600 tons, but the sailing ships were slower than galleys and could not head into the wind. The first ships to do this had lateen sails—triangular sails set lengthwise. This invention probably arrived from the Indian Ocean more than 1,000 years ago. Other eastern inventions included the stern-post rudder and the compass. By 1270, ships' captains also had charts to help them navigate through the Mediterranean and Black seas.

During and after the 1400s, new kinds of ships appeared in the Mediterranean. First came the Portuguese caravel, a two- or three-masted ship with lateen sails. Next was the carrack, probably invented in France. Carracks were large, three-masted merchantmen with square and lateen sails. Similar vessels with gun decks were warships called galleons. In the 1500s, carracks and galleons began sailing across the sea.

Steamships started replacing sailing ships in the nineteenth century. Nowadays, modern ships of all kinds use the Mediterranean, from small fishing boats, yachts, and cabin cruisers to cruise liners, **container ships**, **bulk carriers**, and giant oil tankers. In the early 1990s, Greeks owned more merchant shipping than anyone else in the world.

Above: This fast, sleek Mediterranean ferry carries people and vehicles between Algeciras in Spain and Ceuta, a Spanish town in Morocco.

Trade and Trade Routes

For centuries, the Mediterranean was the world's chief waterway. In time, its main trading centers moved west from Phoenicia and Greece to Italy, Portugal, and Spain.

Phoenician sailors were probably shipping copper from Cyprus to Egypt and Greece 3,500 years ago. By 2,000 years ago, merchant ships traded all around the eastern Mediterranean, calling at ports to take on or unload goods such as wine, almonds, millstones, and iron. In Roman times, ships also carried marble statues and columns from Turkey to Italy and wine, olive oil, cups, and lamps from Italy to France. Spain exported tin, copper, and fish sauce.

Between A.D. 1100 and 1400, Barcelona, Genoa, Venice, and Constantinople (Istanbul) became great shipping centers. Through these ports, grain, wine, and slaves entered Europe

Below: Colorful oarsmen row out into the lagoon of Venice for the Regatta of the Ascension: the feast day when the doge, or leader, would celebrate his city's marriage to the sea.

from Asia. Venetian ships imported precious cargoes of Asian silks, cotton, and spices that had reached the sea overland. Venice exported cloth, glassware, and metalwork.

By A.D. 1500, the great age of Mediterranean sea trade was ending. Portuguese ships began bypassing the Mediterranean and the Venetians and Turks who controlled its trade. The Portuguese learned to sail south around Africa to get spices and silks directly from India and the Far East.

Above: A container ship passes through the Suez Canal, which links the Mediterranean Sea with the Indian Ocean.

Sea trade picked up again after 1869, when the new Suez Canal gave ships a shortcut from Europe to India. More than 100 miles long, this is the world's longest canal, carrying ships of up to 300,000 tons. More than 20,000 vessels use the canal each year. Ships also pass through the narrow Bosporus to the Black Sea and the Strait of Gibraltar to the Atlantic Ocean.

Instead of precious spices and silks, the Mediterranean now carries bulky goods such as iron ore, phosphates, oil, and natural gas. Large amounts of these raw materials and fuels travel from North Africa to Europe. Ships also export manufactured goods from Spain, France, and Italy to various parts of the world.

Most of the Mediterranean's large natural harbors stand on its northern shores. These ports include Barcelona, Marseilles, Genoa, Naples, Venice, Thessaloniki, Piraeus, and Istanbul.

Married to the sea

In the fifth century A.D., refugees from mainland Italy made new homes on low, muddy islands offshore. Their settlement grew into Venice, a city with canals instead of streets. Venice became an independent city-state ruled by nobles, who chose a leader known as the doge. After A.D. 1000, Venice became a great trading sea power with colonies around the east Mediterranean. Once a year, a great festival celebrated the city's success. A procession of galleys rowed out into the lagoon of Venice, and the doge dropped a ring in the water as if marrying Venice to the sea that made it wealthy.

Mineral and Energy Resources

Sea and rocks provide much of the wealth that Mediterranean countries depend on. The main nonliving resources are minerals, oil, and gas from rocks around the sea's rim. Most Mediterranean lands are not rich in minerals, but some have valuable ores of iron, copper, lead, zinc, aluminum, or other metals. For instance, sizable deposits of iron ore crop up in Spain, Algeria, Turkey, and parts of what used to be Yugoslavia. Bauxite (aluminum ore) occurs there and in Greece and France. Bauxite gets its name from Les Baux, a southern French village. Spain has more metals than most Mediterranean countries, while Greece is among those worst off.

Nonmetallic minerals include huge deposits of phosphates, potash, sulfur, and salt used in the chemical industries. Salt comes chiefly from sea water allowed to evaporate in shallow pools on low coasts. Phosphates and potash were laid down on the bed of an ancient sea. Morocco and Tunisia are important phosphate producers, and Israel and Jordan get

Below: Seawater is pumped into a shallow pool in southern Portugal. The sun's heat makes the water evaporate. Salt remains and will be piled into heaps.

Left: Oil flows through pipes from oil wells under the Sahara; waste gas is being burned. Pipes and ships can carry oil and gas from Africa to Europe.

potash and other substances from the very salty, inland Dead Sea. Much of the Mediterranean region also has limestone used for building.

Immense mineral wealth lies unused under the sea. Off southwest Italy, shallow water hides iron ore and manganese deposits produced by volcanoes. Large parts of the sea floor contain layers of rock salt, sulfur, and potash laid down when the Mediterranean almost dried up. There are untapped oil and gas deposits under parts of the continental shelf off Spain, France, Italy, Greece, Turkey, Israel, Egypt, Libya, and Morocco. More oil and gas must lie under sea basins too deep for mining today.

Mediterranean countries generally have poor energy supplies. Outside Spain, few have much coal. But several nations pump oil from wells drilled in the sea-bed offshore, and Algeria and Libya have large, inland reserves of oil and gas. Italy generates much electricity from rivers flowing down from the Alps, but most Mediterranean countries are too dry to generate electricity.

The island of copper

Cyprus has been famous for copper since the Bronze Age. In fact, our word copper comes from *cuprum*, the Latin name that the Romans gave Cyprus. About 5,000 years ago, early metalworkers had found lumps of copper-rich rock lying around on the ground. When they had used these up, teams of slaves began burrowing up to 1,600 ft. into the Troödos Mountains for more. Cyprus yielded about 200,000 tons of copper in 3,000 years. People probably cut down all the forests in Cyprus sixteen times over to get enough wood for fuel to smelt the ore that released this amount of copper.

RESOURCES OF THE MEDITERRANEAN
Living Resources

Almost all Mediterranean countries border the coast, so you might think fish would provide much of their food. In fact, fishing is not that important. The Mediterranean produces only about two percent of the world's total catch. This is because fish are not very plentiful here. Much of the sea lacks the nourishment needed by the tiny organisms that fish depend on for food. Parts of the sea do have plenty of nutrients, though. Good fishing grounds include the shallow waters between Sicily and Tunisia. Boats gather here every year to net schools of big, meaty tuna that arrive from American waters. Mediterranean fishermen also hunt swordfish and surface-swimming schools of little sardines and anchovies. At night, small boats with lamps set out to catch squid. Fishermen find monkfish and skate on the seabed, and there is inshore fishing for crabs, lobsters, prawns, and oysters. Not everything caught is eaten. Divers collect bath sponges and red coral used for making brooches and necklaces.

Most food produced in the Mediterranean region comes not from the sea but from surrounding farmlands. A warm climate means that crops grow year-round. Wheat, barley, and vegetables sprout in the winter. Strawberries ripen early in **polytunnels** in southern Spain. In summer vines produce grapes, and olive trees, olives.

Left: Small boats set out to fish from towns and villages all around the Mediterranean. These two boats are moored just off Karpathos, a Greek island east of Crete.

France, Italy, Spain, and Turkey are among the world's chief grape-growing countries, and much of the world's olive oil (used for cooking) comes from Spain, Italy, Greece, and Turkey. Mediterranean countries have all sorts of tree fruits, including oranges, lemons, figs, pears, peaches, apricots, and various nuts.

On steep slopes, crops grow on terraces—narrow ledges of soil penned in behind rock walls. The largest fields lie on plains and deltas.

Small peasant farmers tend to keep a few sheep or goats for meat and milk. These hardy animals can scramble up rocky mountainsides and eat vegetation too poor for cattle. Donkeys and mules are the main load-carrying animals, but wealthier farmers have replaced animals with pickup trucks.

Above: There is a large orange harvest in Spain, Italy, Israel, and Morocco. Italy, Spain, and Turkey are among the world's chief lemon-growing countries.

RESOURCES OF THE MEDITERRANEAN
Manufacturing

A century ago, large quantities of manufactured goods came from only five Mediterranean cities—Barcelona, Marseilles, Milan, Istanbul, and Alexandria. Their factories still lead the region today. But industries have sprung up in many other places around the coast. One reason is that fuel oil and electricity for powering factory machines are far more plentiful and widespread than they used to be.

Another difference is the goods Mediterranean factories produce. In the 1800s they chiefly turned out woolen, silk, and cotton goods. Egypt, France, and Italy are still big **textile** producers, but in several countries important products now include steel, chemicals, and cars. Wine making, and drying and canning fruit and vegetables also provide employment.

The Mediterranean's two chief manufacturing nations are Italy and Spain. (France's manufacturing cities lie mainly outside the Mediterranean.) Northern Italy imports huge quantities of iron ore to supply the metal industries of Turin

Below: Automated machinery produces sports cars at the Bertone Factory, Turin, in northern Italy. This is one of the Mediterranean's chief car-manufacturing centers.

Left: A Tunisian artist paints designs on tiles used for decorating walls and floors. Old handicrafts still flourish in Islamic countries south and east of the Mediterranean.

and Milan. Turin is a major car-manufacturing city. Milan is the biggest manufacturing center of the entire Mediterranean. Most factories in Milan are small but famous for being up to date and fast. They make everything from farm machinery to china, shoes, medicines, and precision equipment. Northern Italy sells such goods largely to the prosperous countries of nearby Western Europe.

Spain makes steel, machinery, cars, shoes, and textiles. Most Spanish factories are in the northeast, around Barcelona. Manufacturing leaped ahead after Spain joined the **Common Market** in 1986, but Spain has fewer industries than much of Western Europe. Spain's income is derived largely from selling minerals to other European countries.

Manufacturing is less well developed outside Italy and Spain. Although Greece produces textiles, chemicals, and metal products; Turkey makes iron, steel, machinery, and metal products; Egypt turns out textiles and chemicals; and Israel cuts diamonds and makes textiles, electronic equipment, and machinery. Morocco, Algeria, and Tunisia mass-produce superphosphate fertilizer. Like Syria and Turkey, though, they still make carpets, metal articles, and glassware by hand and must buy many manufactured goods from countries with more modern production methods.

RESOURCES OF THE MEDITERRANEAN
Tourism

Its warm, sunny climate makes the Mediterranean coast Europe's most popular vacation playground. From northern Europe, millions of tourists come here each year. Families sunbathe on the beaches and swim or sail in the silky waters. Sports lovers windsurf and play golf. Drivers, cyclists, walkers, and artists enjoy the beautiful scenery. Many older people take luxury cruises. Wildlife attracts bird-watchers and botanists. Art lovers visit old cities, old buildings, and museums.

Different nations offer various attractions. Visitors flock to the beaches of Spain, France, and Turkey. Italy has fine buildings and art treasures, especially in Rome, Florence, and Venice, as well as beaches, magnificent mountains, and lakes. Greece has the historic Acropolis at Athens and many picturesque islands. Israel has Jerusalem, a city holy to Christians, Jews, and Muslims. Egypt is famous for its ancient pyramids and sphinx.

Vacation pay and cheap flights mean that millions of workers from many countries can afford time off anywhere in the Mediterranean area. By the 1980s, Spain was receiving 40 million visitors a year—outnumbering the Spanish population itself. Italy, France, and Greece also attract very large numbers. Other popular Mediterranean destinations include Cyprus, Egypt, Israel, Portugal, and Turkey.

Resorts have sprung up on the coasts to provide vacation accommodations for foreign visitors and vacation or retirement homes. Building for tourism has happened most in Spain. Where only poor fishing villages stood in the 1950s, Spain's Mediterranean shore now bristles with hotels, villas, golf courses, and marinas. This development has provided much work for local people. Thousands have become builders, hotel managers, chefs, waiters and waitresses, tour

Right: Tourists in Turkey admire a Roman temple at Ephesus, an ancient city founded by the Greeks. For many visitors, Greek and Roman ruins are among the Mediterranean's main attractions.

Above: vacationers swim and sunbathe on a beach at Nerja, in southern Spain. Resorts have sprung up all along this stretch of coast, called the Costa del Sol.

guides, bus drivers, and real estate agents. By the 1980s
tourism provided paid work for one in ten Spaniards and was
equal to more than a quarter of Spain's exports. In Cyprus,
tourism earned even more than all the goods sold abroad.

The Sea

The Mediterranean is one of the world's most beautiful seas, but it is also one of the most overused. People catch too many fish and dump too much waste there for the good of the water and its wildlife.

Dumping pollutants—substances that harm the environment—has made the Mediterranean one of the dirtiest seas anywhere. Each year more rubbish pours into its waters from ships, cities, factories, and farms. As cities have grown and factories have multiplied around the coasts, so has their output of wastes. Experts have calculated that every year, the Mediterranean receives up to 60,000 tons of detergents, 12,000 tons of oil, more than 200 tons of chromium, and 100 tons of mercury. On top of these come 500,000 tons of raw sewage from cities and vacation resorts and fertilizers and pesticides washed off fields. Along parts of the northern Mediterranean, enough sewage flows into the sea in one year to form a pile weighing more than 300 tons on every mile of shore.

Once in the sea, wastes cannot disappear quickly because the Mediterranean is surrounded by land. It takes about 100 years before all its water escapes out through the narrow Strait of Gibraltar. So pollutants collect in this sea faster than they are being removed.

Threatened loggerheads

Tourists endanger loggerhead turtles' survival on the Greek island of Zakynthos, one of the reptiles' last breeding grounds in the Mediterranean. Some females are too frightened by vacationers to land to lay eggs in the sandy beaches. Eggs that are laid and covered risk being pierced by beach umbrellas. Hatchlings may fail to dig up through sand packed down by people's feet. Survivors emerging at night can be confused by hotel lights, go the wrong way, and die before finding the sea. Between 1990 and 1995 Zakynthos welcomed more tourists than ever and on one stretch of beach the number of turtles' nests fell by 40 percent.

Below: Sicilian fishermen haul aboard the big tuna fish their nets have trapped. Overfishing has cut the yearly catch to a fraction of what it was.

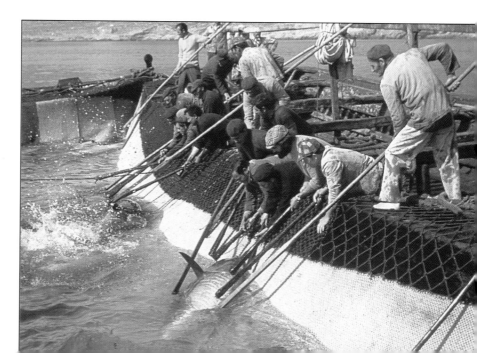

Some areas are more polluted than others. The dirtiest parts are inshore waters off Spain, France, Italy, eastern Greece, Israel, Egypt, and cities on the North African coast. In the northern Adriatic, sewage, fertilizer, and factory wastes sometimes rob water of oxygen, suffocating large numbers of fish. Elsewhere, **sediments** washed off the land have choked and killed sea grasses and soft corals.

Overfishing, overcollecting, and other kinds of human activity also harm life in the Mediterranean. Fishermen have been catching hake, red mullet, sole, and tuna faster than these species can breed. In places, divers have gathered precious coral faster than new coral can grow. In the eastern Mediterranean, disturbance by tourists has badly affected the numbers of monk seals and loggerhead turtles.

Above: Conservationists claimed that metal wastes from this Spanish quarry dissolved in water that poured through an outflow pipe, poisoning the Mediterranean Sea.

EFFECTS ON THE ENVIRONMENT
Mediterranean Lands

Overuse affects not only the sea but also the lands around its rim. Their plants and soils show signs of mistreatment dating back thousands of years. Now, more threats come from tourism and farming. Soon, a new danger could come from the sea.

Below: Goats reach to strip the lower leaves from a small tree. Overgrazing by goats has helped to destroy most of the Mediterranean's forests.

Back in the Stone Age, forests covered many Mediterranean hillsides. Most of these forests have long gone. Overgrazing and felling are mainly to blame for the disappearance of trees. Herds of goats roamed the forests, nibbling and killing young saplings. This left few young trees to replace those that died of old age. Meanwhile, people had been chopping down forests for fuel wood and timber for shipbuilding. More than 250,000 sizable trees probably went to make the warships that fought the Battle of Lepanto in 1571.

As the Mediterranean forests vanished, they were replaced by tough-leaved shrubs and scrawny grasses suited to dry, rocky countryside. In the driest regions, goats or sheep have chewed and killed even these. Where no plant roots remained to hold soil together, the loose soil began blowing away. In parts of southeast Spain and central Turkey such changes have begun turning land into desert.

The large numbers of people who live, work, or take vacations in the region are causing fresh problems. Scattered highrise hotels disfigure large stretches of Spain's coast. In Spain and Israel, farms, hotels, villas, or golf courses use more water from lakes, rivers, or wells than rainfall replaces. In still weather, car fumes produce a hazy smog that poisons the air of cities, especially Athens and Istanbul. Wildlife is suffering too. Each year millions of birds are shot or trapped on migration.

Above: The Adriatic Sea invades St. Mark's Square, Venice. If the city goes on sinking, winter flooding could become more frequent and much more damaging.

Flooding by the sea is the worst risk facing some coasts. Egypt's Nile Delta and Italy's Po Delta are slowly subsiding under the weight of their sediments. During the twentieth century, Venice has sunk more than 9 inches. If the world's climate warms up, polar ice sheets will melt and may raise the sea level everywhere. Then, all the Mediterranean's deltas and low coastal plains will drown.

EFFECTS ON THE ENVIRONMENT
Environmental Problems and People

Overuse and misuse of water, land, and air are making life harder for some Mediterranean peoples.

The sea is less rich in food than it used to be. By the 1980s, **overfishing** had cut Sicily's tuna harvest from 10,000 to a few hundred. Sardine schools have vanished off the Nile Delta because the Nile River no longer pours nutrients into the sea. These are trapped upriver in Lake Nasser, which was formed when the Aswan High Dam blocked the river's main flow. Mediterranean shellfish are not always as safe to eat as they were. Sewage or chemical wastes **contaminate** them in more than nine out of ten areas where they are caught.

Water pollution and air pollution cause health problems too. Germs in sewage polluting some inshore waters put people who bathe there at risk of catching diseases. Some coasts get filthy enough to drive tourists away; keeping them clean is expensive. Meanwhile, the smogs that choke Athens and Istanbul can cause breathing complaints.

As Mediterranean people multiply, they need more freshwater and land to live and grow food on. But there is a limit to these things. In parts of Spain, water is often rationed, and where buildings or deserts invade fields, cropland disappears. In Egypt the Aswan High Dam and Lake Nasser are largely to blame. The vast lake drowns farms and traps sediments that the Nile would have carried downstream to fertilize fields and add to the Nile Delta. Now the fields are

Right: Between Athens and the blue sky hangs a dirty haze produced by car and truck exhausts. This photochemical smog stings people's eyes and causes breathing problems.

Below: Immigrants from North Africa buy and sell at a street market in the French capital, Paris. Many thousands of poor Algerians have moved to France, which once ruled Algeria.

less fertile than they were, and the sea gnaws away the edge of the delta.

If the sea level rises, people on all low coasts will suffer. The Mediterranean might rise 3 ft. by the year 2050. That would harm one in five people living near the shore. Much of the Nile Delta's farmland would drown, and millions of Egyptians could starve.

Even without this disaster, poverty has driven many people abroad to find work. Thousands of Turks went to Germany, and many Algerians now work and live in France.

Scum in the Adriatic

In 1989, northern Adriatic coasts were choked by rotting algae and foam up to 33 feet thick. The causes were sewage, fertilizers, and factory chemicals washed off the land. Some of these substances nourished marine algae. In hot summer weather, the filmy water plants multiplied fast. Then they began to die off. The **bacteria** that made the dead algae rot also took oxygen out of the water. Many sea creatures suffocated. The result was a smelly mess that spoiled beaches and drove away tourists from some of Italy's most popular holiday resorts. Each summer the same problem threatens to recur.

EFFECTS ON THE ENVIRONMENT
Remedies

In 1976, seventeen Mediterranean nations agreed to the United Nations Mediterranean Action Plan to stop wastes damaging the sea. They promised to ban oil dumping and to prevent new factories letting chemicals poison the water.

Since 1976, France has fitted equipment to remove nine-tenths of the pollution from its huge **petrochemical plant** and steelworks near the mouth of the Rhône River. By the 1980s, Athens, Marseilles, and Naples were planning or installing systems to stop untreated sewage entering the sea. Athens limited the use of cars in the city to reduce its smog.

Tourist areas began making special efforts to clean up. Boats, called pelicans, collect rubbish floating in the sea off Nice, in southern France. Venice dredges a million tons of algae a year from its lagoon before the algae rots and stinks. Spain now has laws to stop builders spoiling the coast.

Countries have passed laws protecting wildlife. For example, Tunisia stops trawlers hunting in shallow water where many fish spawn. This gives young fish the chance to grow. Greek

Below: Irrigating crops uses more water than dry countries can obtain from wells or rivers. Using water from sewage is one way of tackling this water shortage.

Left: Conservationists sometimes fence off turtle-nesting beaches and move turtles' eggs at risk of being dug up or damaged. This turtle project was photographed in Cyprus.

regulations forbid people to disturb the turtle beaches of the island of Zakynthos. Also, conservationists campaign to stop Mediterranean hunters killing migrating birds.

Several countries have tackled fresh water shortages. Israel has irrigated farms with water from recycled sewage and from dew trickling from stones heaped around fruit trees. In the 1990s, Jordan planned to use electricity to turn saltwater into freshwater as it flowed through a canal from the Red Sea to refill the inland Dead Sea. The Dead Sea was drying up because Israeli farms took water from the Jordan River, which supplies it.

Engineers have designed giant gates to protect Venice from sudden surges in sea level. By the mid-1990s, however, no gates had been constructed, and there were no plans to stop deltas drowning if the entire Mediterranean sea level rose.

Many schemes for saving the environment remain wishful thinking. Some countries cannot afford to cure their own pollution. Some seem unwilling or unable to enforce wildlife conservation laws. But at least improvements have begun.

Glossary

algae Simple water plants.

anticyclones Masses of high-pressure air that tend to bring still, settled weather.

bacteria Tiny living things including kinds that cause dead plants and animals to decay.

barbarians Peoples thought of as uncivilized by the Romans whose lands they conquered.

Bronze Age A time when people used bronze tools and weapons. It came after the Stone Age and before the Iron Age.

bulk carriers A big cargo ship designed to carry large, loose loads such as iron ore.

canyons Steep-sided gullies or valleys.

colonists Settlers in a new country forming a community.

Common Market An economic and political association of certain European countries as a unit.

container ships Cargo ships that carry goods prepacked in large, standard-sized boxes.

contaminate To spoil an environment with a pollutant.

continental shelf The submerged edge of a continent sloping gently to a depth of about 650 feet.

crusades Christian expeditions to Palestine to try to retake Jesus' homeland from the Muslims.

crust The earth's hard, rocky outer layer.

crustaceans Creatures in the group of invertebrates that includes crabs, lobsters, and shrimps.

currents An ocean current is a "river in the sea."

depressions Masses of low-pressure air that tend to bring wet windy weather.

food web An imaginary web made up of connected food chains. Each of its food chains has creatures that eat or are eaten by creatures in another food chain.

invertebrates Animals without backbones.

Iron Age The time when people made and used iron tools and weapons. It came after the Bronze Age.

lagoon A shallow area of salt water usually separated from the open sea by a narrow strip of land.

mistral A strong north wind in southern France. It sometimes blows down the Rhône Valley to the Mediterranean Sea.

mollusks Creatures in the group of invertebrates that includes snails, clams, squid, and octopuses.

Neanderthal A stocky type of prehistoric human being that lived mainly in Europe during the Ice Age.

overfishing Catching fish faster than those that remain can breed to replace them.

petrochemical plant A factory that uses oil or gas to make chemicals such as plastics, medicines, and synthetic rubber.

Phoenician Seafaring people who once lived on the coasts of what are now Syria, Lebanon, and Israel.

plankton Plants and animals that drift about in surface waters. Most are very tiny.

pollution Something that poisons land, sea, or air.

polytunnels Polyethylene tunnels covering crops to keep them warm and speed growth.

sediments Sand, silt, or other substances that have settled on the bed of a lake, river, or sea.

Stone Age The time before people began making metal tools and weapons.

strait A narrow strip of sea linking two larger sea areas.

tectonic plates The great slabs of rock forming the earth's hard outer surface.

textile A woven, knitted or other fabric made of wool, cotton, or nylon.

Further Information

BOOKS TO READ:

Arnold, Francis. *Greece*. World in View. Austin, TX: Raintree Steck-Vaughn, 1992.

Brill, Marlene Targ. *Libya*. Enchantment of the World. Chicago: Children's Press, 1987.

Coldrey, Jennifer. *Life in the Sea*. The Sea. New York: Bookwright Press, 1991.

Gay, Kathlyn. *Water Pollution*. Impact Books. New York: Franklin Watts, 1990.

Harris, Colin. *Protecting the Planet*. Young Geographer. New York: Thomson Learning, 1993.

Morris, Scott, ed. *Industry of the World*. New York: Chelsea House, 1993.

Travis, David. *The Land and People of Italy*. New York: HarperCollins Children's Books, 1992.

CD ROMS:

Geopedia: The Multimedia Geography CD-Rom. Chicago: Encyclopedia Britannica.

Habitats. Austin, TX: Raintree Steck-Vaughn, 1996.

USEFUL ADDRESSES:

Center for Environmental Education
Center for Marine Conservation
1725 De Sales Street NW
Suite 500
Washington, DC 20036

Environmental Defense Fund
1616 P Street NW
Suite 150
Washington, DC 20036

World Wildlife Fund
1250 24th Street NW
Washington, DC 20037

Index